St. Louis

St. Louis

A Downtown America Book

Barbara Ford

dP Dillon Press, Inc.   Minneapolis, MN 55415

Library of Congress Cataloging-in-Publication Data

Ford, Barbara.
    St. Louis / Barbara Ford.
       p.   cm. — (A Downtown America book)
    Includes index.
    Summary: Explores the city recognized as the nation's busiest
inland river port, describing its history, neighborhoods, and
points of interest.
    ISBN 0-87518-402-2
    1. Saint Louis (Mo.)—Juvenile literature. [1. Saint Louis
(Mo.)]
I. Title. II. Title: Saint Louis. III. Series.
F474.S24F66 1989
977.8'66—dc 19   88-35912
                                    CIP
                                     AC

Dillon Press, Inc., 242 Portland Avenue South
Minneapolis, Minnesota 55415

Printed in the United States of America
1 2 3 4 5 6 7 8 9 10 98 97 96 95 94 93 92 91 90 89

Photographic Acknowledgments

The photographs are reproduced through the courtesy of Anheuser Busch; Day Photo; Barbara Ford; Robert Lee II (© Robert Lee II, pages 2, 10, 13, 24, 26, 38); the Missouri Botanical Garden; the Missouri Historical Society; and the National Park Service, Department of the Interior.

Contents

Fast Facts about St. Louis

St. Louis: The Gateway to the West; Lion of the Valley; the River City

Location: West bank of Mississippi River, east central Missouri

Area: City, 61 square miles (158 square kilometers); metropolitan area, 3,176 square miles (8,226 square kilometers)

Population (1986 estimate*): City, 426,300; metropolitan area, 2,438,000

Major Population Groups: Blacks, Germans, English, Irish

Altitude: 455 feet (138.8 meters) above sea level

Climate: Average temperature is 33°F (1°C) in January, 81°F (27°C) in July; average annual precipitation, including rain and snow, is 35.3 inches (90.7 centimeters)

Founding Date: 1764, incorporated as a city in 1822

City Flag: A red background with two wavy white and blue bars representing the Mississippi and Missouri rivers and a fleur-de-lis representing France

City Seal: Steamboat on the Mississippi River

Form of Government: Mayor-council; mayor and 28 members and president of the Board of Aldermen are elected to four-year terms

Important Industries: Transportation, chemical research, health care, beer brewing

*U.S. Bureau of the Census 1988 population estimates available in fall 1989; official 1990 census figures available in 1991-92.

Festivals and Parades

February/March: Mardi Gras Parade, Soulard

March: St. Patrick's Day Parade (and Run), downtown

May: St. Louis Storytelling Festival, Jefferson National Expansion Memorial; Tilles Park Craft Fair

June: Annual National Ragtime and Classic Jazz Festival, *Goldenrod* Showboat

July: Independence Day/Veiled Prophet Fair, Jefferson National Expansion Memorial; Strassenfest (German Festival), downtown; Annual Fire Engine Rally, Jefferson Memorial, Forest Park

August/September: Japanese Festival, Shaw's Garden

September: Great Forest Park Balloon Race, Forest Park

December: Christmas Parade, downtown

For further information about festivals and parades, see agencies listed on page 56.

United States

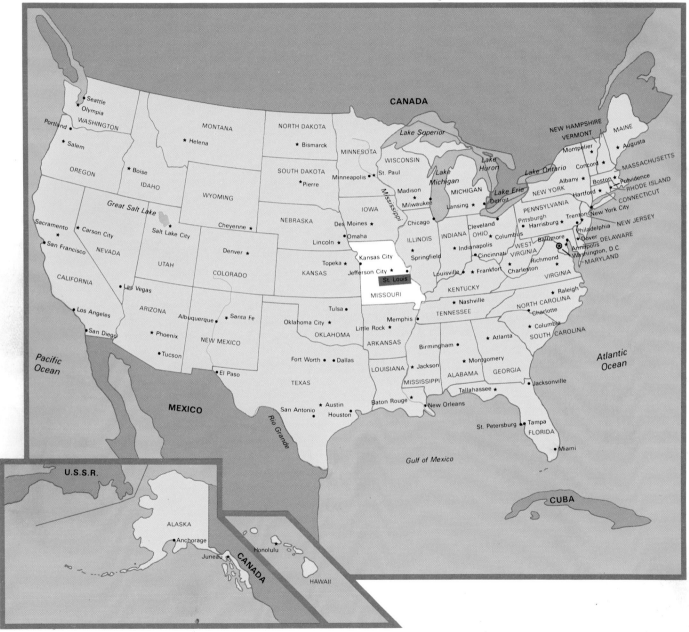

St. Louis

MISSOURI
St. Louis

Points of Interest

1. Jefferson National Expansion Memorial
   (Gateway Arch, Old Cathedral, Old Courthouse)
2. Ead's Bridge
3. Laclede's Landing
4. Anheuser-Busch Brewery
5. Campbell House
6. Missouri Botanical (Shaw's) Garden
7. Busch Memorial Stadium
8. St. Louis Art Museum
9. St. Louis Zoo
10. Jefferson Memorial Building
11. McDonnell Planetarium
12. Grant's Farm
13. Lock No. 27

ST. LOUIS

Central West End
Forest Park
Midtown
Hyde Park
Lafayette Park
The Hill
Tower Grove Park
Soulard
Carondelet
Carondelet Park

MISSOURI
ILLINOIS

CHAIN OF ROCKS CANAL
MISSISSIPPI RIVER
MARK TWAIN EXPRESSWAY
BROADWAY
WEST FLORISSANT AVENUE
NATURAL BRIDGE ROAD
UNION BOULEVARD
MARTIN LUTHER KING BOULEVARD
DELMAR BOULEVARD
GRAND BOULEVARD
JEFFERSON AVENUE
DANIEL BOONE EXPRESSWAY
MANCHESTER AVENUE
KINGSHIGHWAY BOULEVARD
HAMPTON AVENUE
I-44
I-70
I-55
CHIPPEWA STREET
GRAVOIS AVENUE
BROADWAY

ST. LOUIS COUNTY
CITY OF ST. LOUIS

N

0   2   miles 3½
0   2   3½ kilometers

1

Gateway to the West

St. Louis's Gateway Arch, the tallest monument in the United States, towers 630 feet (192 meters) over the city. The shining steel arch was named in honor of the city's role as Gateway to the West in pioneer days. Starting from the place where the arch now stands, the pioneers went west by steamboat and wagon. Today, the arch offers the best view of modern St. Louis. A special train in each leg of the arch carries visitors up to a room near the top, where on a clear day they can see for as far as 30 miles (48 kilometers).

The Mississippi River, the longest river in North America, flows below the arch. At St. Louis it is 2,000 feet (610 meters) wide and a muddy brown color. From the arch, the city of St. Louis spreads out along the Mississippi for 19 miles (31 kilometers) to

The Gateway Arch in downtown St. Louis rises above the Mississippi riverfront.

the south and north. Across the river lies Illinois, which is linked to St. Louis by the three graceful arches of Eads Bridge and other newer bridges. Barges—long, flat boats—are pushed by towboats up and down the river night and day.

The area visitors see from the top of the arch is the fourteenth largest metropolitan area in the United States. It includes the city of St. Louis, St. Louis County, and parts of other counties in Missouri and Illinois. More than 2.4 million people live in this area.

Although the St. Louis metropolitan area is one of the largest in the country, the city of St. Louis covers only 61 square miles (158 square kilometers). That is the smallest geographic area of any major U.S. city. St. Louis County, which surrounds the city on the south, north, and west, has a much larger area and twice as many people. The city and the county separated back in 1876, when city dwellers thought they were being taxed unfairly by a joint city-county government. Today the city regrets the split, but it is still a fact.

People in both the city and the county must cope with summers that can be very hot and humid. Such weather is caused in part by the city's location on the Mississippi River, 1,000 miles (1,610 kilometers) upriver from the Gulf of Mexico. During the summer, moist, warm air moves up from the gulf. The Mississippi and Missouri rivers contribute moisture to

Riverboats dock along the Mississippi beneath the arches of Eads Bridge.

The Mississippi River a short distance upstream from downtown St. Louis.

the St. Louis area, too. Scientists think that the gulf air also plays a role in the tornados that sometimes threaten the city in the spring and fall.

St. Louis's location, and the people who live there, reflect a history that goes back more than two centuries.

The city was founded in the eighteenth century by Frenchmen who moved up the Mississippi River from what was then the French colony of Louisiana. In the nineteenth century, many German immigrants came to St. Louis, and Germans became the city's largest national group. Today, though, black St. Louisans outnumber the members of any one national group.

The first business in St. Louis, the fur trade, made many of the city's early residents wealthy. During the 1800s, St. Louis became a center for a variety of industries. In the mid 1860s, two St. Louisans of German descent took over a bankrupt brewery and built it into the world's largest brewery, Anheuser-Busch. About the same time, three St. Louis brothers, the Mallinckrodts, established a chemical plant that has grown into a world-famous firm. The Monsanto Company and a leading food company, Ralston Purina, both began long ago in St. Louis, too.

McDonnell Douglas Corporation,

A Monsanto scientist observes the growth of experimental plants.

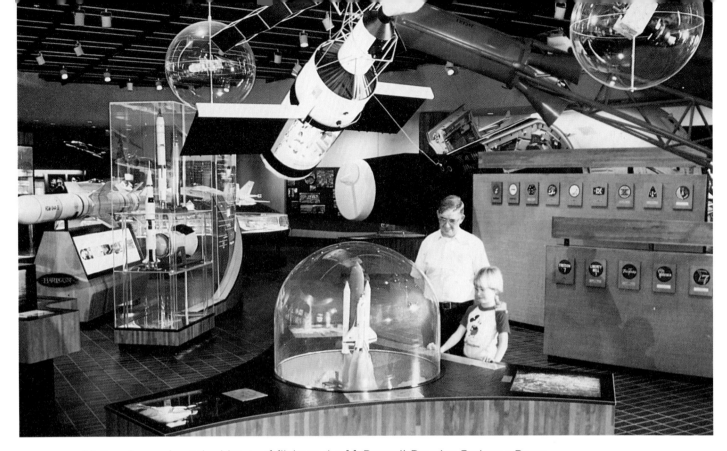

Visitors learn about the history of flight at the McDonnell Douglas Prologue Room.

which makes aircraft and spacecraft, arrived in St. Louis much later but is now the area's biggest employer. Its headquarters are in St. Louis County, next to Lambert-St. Louis Airport. The McDonnell Douglas Prologue Room, which tells the story of flight, displays full-size models of Mercury and Gemini spacecraft.

Today, the St. Louis area has more than three thousand manufacturing plants that make products ranging from shoes to steel. The three biggest U.S. automakers—General Motors,

Ford, and Chrysler—have plants in St. Louis, where they make more cars than in any other U.S. city except Detroit.

St. Louis's central location helps make it a good place for business. Products travel from St. Louis to points all over the United States. Other products arrive in the city from the west and north and are shipped onward to their final destination. They are moved by river barge, truck, rail, and air. In fact, St. Louis is a center for all four kinds of transportation.

Still, St. Louis is best known as a river port—the second busiest inland river port in the United States. Once St. Louis was the "queen city of steamboating." The steamboats are gone now, but each year thousands of barges pushed by towboats dock at the huge Port of St. Louis.

Through its transportation network, St. Louis is still a gateway city—a gateway to cities and towns all over the United States.

2

The River City

St. Louis is a river city. Every day, from 50 to 100 barges unload and load their cargos in the Port of St. Louis. Since St. Louis is the northernmost port on the Mississippi where there is usually no ice during the winter, it stays open to river traffic throughout the year.

The river was where it all began, more than two hundred years ago. In 1763, Pierre Laclede Liguest and Auguste Chouteau floated down the Mississippi in wooden boats. They were looking for a place to establish a fur trading post. About 18 miles (29 kilometers) below the point where the Missouri River joins the Mississippi, they saw a promising site where a hill sloped down to a high bluff.

After inspecting the site, Laclede decided to establish the new trading post there. It would be called St.

River traffic in the busy Port of St. Louis.

Louis, for the patron saint of their king, Louis XV of France.

For many years after that, most of the people who lived in St. Louis were French. They had names such as Gratiot, Labbadie, Soulard, and Lucas—names that still appear on street signs and city maps. Yet St. Louis actually belonged to Spain until that country transferred a huge tract of land called the Louisiana Territory to France. St. Louis was part of the tract. Only a few years later, in 1803, France sold the Louisiana Territory to the United States. Historians have called the Louisiana Purchase the best real estate deal the United States ever made.

President Thomas Jefferson needed information about the vast area, so he sent two U.S. army officers, Meriwether Lewis and William Clark, on an expedition through the Louisiana Territory. The men started their voyage in St. Louis, where they bought supplies and met the town's leading citizens. Two years later, the expedition returned to St. Louis. In the house of Pierre Chouteau, Auguste's brother, Lewis and Clark wrote the first reports of their journey.

The Lewis and Clark expedition fired people's imagination, and soon many Americans were moving west. Some of them never went beyond St. Louis. Others made St. Louis their starting point. They bought food, wagons, horses, boats, and other supplies and moved on to the vast frontier west of the Mississippi. Though the fur trade was still St. Louis's main

The *Golden Eagle* was the last stern-wheeled, wooden-hulled packet steamer on the Mississippi.

business, many of its citizens began to make their living supplying pioneers with the goods they needed to travel west. St. Louis had become the Gateway to the West.

In 1817, the *Zebulon M. Pike* steamed upriver to St. Louis and start-ed a new period in the city's history. One of the first steamboats, the *Pike* had come all the way from the eastern United States. Before long, St. Louis became the leading steamboat port in the nation. From its port, boats could travel north and south on the

Mississippi River, and west and east on rivers that flowed into the Mississippi. In 1857, a reporter described the waterfront scene in St. Louis: "A mile of steamboats. Hundreds of drays, wagons, and carriages rushing along at all speed."

Mark Twain, the Missouri-born author of *Tom Sawyer* and *Huckleberry Finn*, was one of the river pilots who guided steamboats in those busy days. He earned his pilot's certificate in St. Louis in 1859.

The city's reign as steamboat queen was short. In 1874, engineer James B. Eads designed a bridge that would carry railroad cars as well as wagons across the river at St. Louis. It was Eads's first bridge, and many wondered whether it could bear the weight of heavy railroad cars.

To calm their fears, Eads tested the bridge's strength. First, he sent a locomotive over the structure, and then an elephant. Finally, he directed fourteen locomotives to pull cars loaded with coal to the center of the bridge. When the locomotives made the trip safely, everyone cheered.

Eads Bridge helped make St. Louis one of the leading rail centers in the United States. Anheuser-Busch designed special refrigerated rail cars to carry its beer all over the country. Railroads created new markets for Anheuser-Busch and St. Louis industry—but not for steamboats. In the 1880s, Mark Twain visited the St. Louis levee where so many steamboats had once docked and found only a few

Large crowds came to see the attractions of St. Louis's 1904 World's Fair.

left. Trains had replaced the boats.

In 1904, the St. Louis World's Fair, also called the Louisiana Purchase Exposition, was held in Forest Park. This celebration marked the 100th anniversary of the Louisiana Purchase. The fair was a big success and is still considered one of the finest ever held. It introduced the ice cream cone and iced tea to the world. A popular song, *Meet Me in St. Louis*, was written about the fair, and a movie with the same title, starring Judy Garland, used the fair as the background.

A towboat pushes barges loaded with coal along the Mississippi at St. Louis.

During World War I, Mississippi River traffic made a comeback. The U.S. government realized that one way to move goods quickly and cheaply was by barges—low, flat boats pushed by towboats. The towboats and barges did such a good job during the war that they continued to be used on the river in peacetime.

Today, modern diesel towboats push barges that carry products such as grain, coal, and cement. But instead of docking at the foot of the old levee in downtown St. Louis, as steamboats did, tows (the name for a towboat and its barges) use docks scattered along the river for 70 miles (113 kilometers). This whole area is known as the Port of St. Louis.

After the docks were moved away from the St. Louis riverfront, much of the downtown area became a slum. Near the river, rundown warehouse and apartment buildings surrounded the beautiful Old Cathedral, completed in 1834, and the grand Old Courthouse, finished in 1862. Few people visited these reminders of St. Louis's past.

Yet the riverfront as it once was lived on in the hearts of a few St. Louisans. One of them was Luther Ely Smith, a wealthy lawyer. Smith talked about his dream to anyone who would listen, and in 1934, he saw it begin to come true. The U.S. Congress created a federal commission to plan a memorial at the site of old St. Louis. Smith was named a member of the commission. "Make no small plans," Professor Charles E. Merriman advised his fellow members as they began to consider what to do with the riverfront.

They took his advice and came up with a plan that included a museum, a park, and a memorial, as well as the Old Courthouse and Old Cathedral. Smith raised a quarter of a million dollars as a prize for the best design for a memorial.

The contest was won by architect Eero Saarinen, who designed a steel arch that would be a symbol of St. Louis as the Gateway to the West.

Some people joked that the plans for the arch looked like a croquet wicket. But when the shining 630-foot (192-meter) steel arch was finished in 1965, just about everyone liked it.

The Gateway Arch, the Museum of Western Expansion in its basement, the park surrounding the arch, and the Old Cathedral and Old Courthouse make up the Jefferson National Expansion Memorial National Park. It is one of the most popular tourist attractions in the country.

The success of the memorial changed the whole riverfront. Old buildings were restored, and new buildings constructed. Instead of moving away from the river, people began moving back. The baseball Cardinals, winners of three National League pennants in the 1980s, now play in a new stadium a short distance from the arch. Every year in early July, St. Louis hosts the nation's biggest Independence Day celebration at the Jefferson National Expansion Memorial.

In St. Louis, you can go back to the river, where it all began.

Fireworks light up the sky by the Gateway Arch.

3

Brick Homes and Private Places

Even though the city of St. Louis isn't very big, it has a wide variety of neighborhoods. In the mid-1800s, St. Louisans began moving away from the crowded, noisy riverfront. A dozen blocks west, they built St. Louis's first neighborhood, Lucas Place. Robert Campbell, a wealthy fur trader, bought a fine house for his family in this part of the city. Today, Campbell House is a museum and the only building that remains from Lucas Place. One room of the house displays the Campbell children's toys.

Other early neighborhoods still exist. Just south of downtown is Lafayette Park, an area where wealthy St. Louisans built large houses in the 1830s and 1840s. In 1896, a tornado blew down every tree in the park. The trees were replaced, and later the area around the park—Lafayette Square—

A house in one of St. Louis's "private places" in the Central West End.

became the city's first historic district. Today well-to-do St. Louisans once again live in the square's tall, elegant houses. And once more the park is a center of activity for everything from dog walking to softball.

Another early neighborhood, Soulard, borders the Lafayette area. Unlike Lafayette Square, it is an area of mostly small homes, built by the German immigrants who began to settle in St. Louis in the 1830s. Some of the companies at which the immigrants worked, such as Anheuser-Busch, are still in Soulard. Although this neighborhood once became a slum, it is now a well-preserved historic district. Here middle-class St. Louisans live in small and medium-sized brick homes that have been lovingly restored.

Campbell House.

A restored room at Campbell House displays toys from Lucas Place in the mid-1800s.

A good time to visit Soulard is Saturday morning, when the open-air market near Lafayette Avenue is at its peak. It sells the best fruits and vegetables in the city, as well as a variety of other merchandise.

Soulard and Lafayette Park form a small part of South St. Louis, a sprawling area of wide, straight streets, sturdy brick buildings, and parks. One of the most attractive sections was created by Henry Shaw, a wealthy hardware merchant who died in 1889. He gave the site of the Missouri Botanical Garden, known as Shaw's Garden, and the neighboring site of Tower Grove Park to the city. Today, the neighborhoods around the park and the garden offer a variety of housing: large houses, small houses, apartment buildings, and multi-family buildings called "flats."

On any day of the year, many residents of this area can be found in Tower Grove Park and Shaw's Garden. The park has a family fitness course, tennis courts, bike paths, a pond, and several playgrounds. St. Louisans enjoy gathering in its brightly painted picnic shelters, which were designed by Henry Shaw's British architect. Each one is different. The architect also designed a bandshell, where musical groups give concerts on Monday evenings in the summer.

The best-known feature of Shaw's Garden is the Climatron, a huge, domed greenhouse that houses tropical plants. A walk through the Climatron guides visitors through different tropical climates, each with its own plants. The garden also has the nation's oldest greenhouse and largest Japanese garden. Children like to stand on the curved bridge over the pond in the Japanese garden and drop food to the carp (a very large relative of the goldfish). Shaw's Garden was Henry Shaw's estate; his home and tomb are both on the grounds.

Shaw's Garden and Tower Grove Park are close to two of the best-known places in St. Louis—the Ted Drewes frozen custard stands. Here Drewes serves his famous creation, the

The Climatron at Shaw's Garden houses many varieties of tropical plants.

"concrete," which has the texture of wet concrete. This cold, creamy treat is as filling as a whole meal.

The oldest part of South St. Louis is Carondelet. Founded in the 1770s as a separate village, it became part of St. Louis in 1870. Carondelet's small

Bellerive Park lies on a bluff overlooking the Mississippi. From here, the sandbars and woods on the Illinois side appear much as they must have looked in 1764. The neighborhood's other park, big Carondelet Park, is popular with young people. Younger

A house in St. Louis's Hill neighborhood.

children use the playground, and older ones fish the park's lakes.

One section of South St. Louis lacks everything the other neighborhoods have. The Hill, St. Louis's Italian neighborhood, doesn't have beautiful architecture, parks, or views. Yet the Hill, settled around 1900, has other things that make it special—rows of narrow, neat frame houses with fences, brickface, woodwork, religious statues, and flags. Hill residents can often be seen painting, planting, and improving their small properties.

Amighetti's, which sells delicious homemade Italian ice cream, is a favorite spot for Hill residents and other St. Louisans. On weekend afternoons in the summer, a band plays in the outdoor garden.

A young visitor gets a close-up view of a puppet at Bob Kramer's Marionnettes.

Grand Boulevard, a main street, runs north from South St. Louis to the area known as Midtown. St. Louis University, the city's oldest and the first university west of the Mississippi, is on North Grand, along with Powell Hall, home of the St. Louis Symphony. Also on Grand is the Fox Theatre, a restored 1928 "movie palace" which now presents theatrical events. Midtown is the home of Bob Kramer's Marionnettes, where many young people come to see exciting demonstrations of puppetry.

West of Midtown is the Central West End, where many wealthy citizens moved when older neighborhoods became crowded. In the Central West End, they invented a special kind of neighborhood, the private place. Each is guarded by two huge gates, one of which is closed to keep out through traffic. Most private places still exist, and wealthy St. Louisans still live in these quiet areas close to busy city streets. On Portland and Westmoreland Place, the huge mansions, each set in a broad lawn, look like palaces.

Most of the Central West End isn't as quiet or grand as the private places, but it does have many handsome houses and apartment buildings on broad streets. Poet T.S. Eliot and playwright Tennessee Williams grew up on Westminster Street. Williams set his famous play, *The Glass Menagerie*, in his house at 4633 Westminster. Lindell Boulevard has the New Cathedral, the city's largest Catholic church. Inside, the ceiling and walls are covered with shimmering mosaics made of tiny pieces of colored stone. Euclid Street has fine shops and restaurants.

North St. Louis has a higher percentage of low-income people than other areas of the city. It was the site of a housing project, Pruett-Igoe, that was one of the worst failures in public housing. There were so many complaints about the project that eventually it had to be torn down. Yet North St. Louis has very successful housing projects, too, such as Coch-

ran Gardens. Managed by its own tenants, Cochran has had such a good record that people come from all over the country to study its success.

While South St. Louis has its Drewes frozen custard stands, North St. Louis has an equally famous institution, Crown Candy Kitchen. St. Louisans have been buying ice cream and candy in this modest little building since 1913. Inside, its old wooden booths and fixtures and its colorful antique juke box look much the same as they did in the early part of the twentieth century.

It's not far from Crown Candy Kitchen to a historic area, Hyde Park. Fine nineteenth-century brick houses, some of them restored, line the streets. The Black Repertory Theater is located in Hyde Park, as is the oldest house in St. Louis, the 1830 Bissell Mansion.

St. Louisans are very proud of their neighborhoods. Every one has a special banner or sign, which is hung from street lamps or other structures. Associations in each of the neighborhoods work with the city government to keep their areas clean and safe and to provide parks and playgrounds. Neighborhoods make St. Louis an interesting and vibrant city.

Seeing St. Louis

There are many places to have fun in St. Louis, but today the riverfront is the first place people go to find enjoyable things to see and do. The Jefferson National Expansion Memorial is the riverfront's leading attraction, and it has much more to offer than just the view from the top of the Gateway Arch. In the underground space beneath the arch is the largest museum in a national park, the Museum of Westward Expansion. It tells the story of how the west was explored and settled.

The Old Cathedral and the Old Courthouse are both part of the memorial. In the Old Cathedral, the bell that rang in the first church on this site—the church attended by Pierre Laclede and Auguste Chouteau—is on display. The Old Courthouse has exhibits that tell the story of St. Louis, in

In this view, the Gateway Arch rises over the Old Courthouse.

which the Old Courthouse played an important part. Here Dred Scott, a slave, filed a lawsuit to be declared free. Though he lost his case in the famous Dred Scott Decision, soon the Civil War began which ended slavery in the United States.

The grounds of the memorial slope down to the Mississippi, bordered by the old cobblestone levee. A dozen boats are moored here, ranging from the only floating Burger King to the *President*, the nation's largest excursion boat. The fat, shiny boat is the steel-covered *Admiral*, a 1940 excursion vessel that now serves as an entertainment center. The old wooden boat is a real showboat, the 1909 *Goldenrod*, on which shows are still performed every night.

The *City of St. Louis*, a real towboat, once pushed barges up and down the Mississippi between St. Louis and New Orleans. Today it houses the St. Louis Visitors Center and a gift shop. Visitors can tour the ship's crew quarters, the galley, the engine room, and the pilot house high above the river. In the pilot house, a tape plays the voices of real river pilots talking as they guide their vessels. Actually, this boat, like many others nearby, no longer leaves the dock.

One of the best places to get a close-up view of towboats pushing barges is across the river, in Granite City, Illinois. Lock 27, the last lock on the Mississippi as boats go south (and the first one as they go north), is located on a canal built so that boats can

The Old Courthouse forms one part of the Jefferson National Expansion Memorial.

Today the *City of St. Louis* attracts many visitors who want to learn about life on a riverboat.

bypass a dangerous stretch of the river next to North St. Louis. The U.S. Army Corps of Engineers, which is responsible for keeping the river channel open, operates a small visitors center at Lock 27.

Another part of the St. Louis riverfront scene lies just north of the arch. In the mid-nineteenth century, this area was covered with warehouses and other businesses that served the steamboats. Now it is a historic district known as Laclede's Landing, and the warehouses are shops, restaurants, and

River traffic lines up at Lock 27.

offices. Here visitors are entertained and informed at the Dental Health Theater, which uses puppets and giant teeth to tell the story of dental health.

St. Louis's major league baseball team, the Cardinals, has returned to the river to play in Busch Stadium, a few blocks west of the arch. Baseball fans can take a guided tour which allows them to sit in the Cardinals' dugout and stand on the playing field. The St. Louis Sports Hall of Fame is located in the stadium, and the National Bowling Hall of Fame is across the street.

Five blocks north of Busch Stadium is the new St. Louis Centre. This mall has a vaulted glass roof and landscaping that make shoppers feel as if they are in a greenhouse. Even more eye-catching is the huge new St. Louis Union Station in what was once the city's main railway station. It has shops, restaurants, a hotel, and a lake with small boats.

Across the street from the station stands a St. Louis landmark, the fountain called *Meeting of the Waters*. Sculpted by Carl Milles, it shows the Mississippi River as a man on a catfish giving a flower to the Missouri River, a woman.

Except for the riverfront, Forest Park, the third-largest city park in the nation, has more attractions than any any other part of St. Louis. When it opened in 1876, the park was a long ride by horse and carriage from downtown. Now St. Louisans get there on a short trip by car or bus. Forest Park

Balloons rise in front of Union Station.

was once a forest, but the park was completely landscaped for the 1904 World's Fair. To make room for new buildings and exhibits, many trees were cut down.

The St. Louis Art Museum was one of the World's Fair buildings. Today a new wing houses a gift shop with a special section for young people. Across the street is a bronze statue of the saint for whom the city was named—a copy of the statue that stood at the fair's entrance. The large lake below the art museum is the same lake over which boats glided during the fair. Visitors can rent rowboats, canoes, and electric boats for use on the lake.

A short distance from the art museum is the huge open-air bird cage built for the fair. Now part of the St. Louis Zoo, the cage is 228 feet (69.5 meters) long, 84 feet (25.7 meters) wide, and 50 feet (15.2 meters) high. A walkway allows visitors to stroll through it. The zoo, one of the best in the country, was a pioneer in the use of enclosures that provide animals with homes similar to the ones they have in the wild. The "rocks" in many of the exhibits are really made from a substance that has been molded to look like rock. A children's zoo has animals that can be petted and a nursery where baby animals are displayed.

Money left over from the fair was used to build Jefferson Memorial Building, which houses the History Museum. One exhibit is devoted to Charles Lindbergh, whose *Spirit of St.*

Charles Lindbergh stands next to his famous plane, *Spirit of St. Louis*, on May 11, 1927.

Louis was the first airplane to cross the Atlantic Ocean. Lindbergh lived in St. Louis for a time, and St. Louisans financed the plane. Though the *Spirit* is now displayed in the Smithsonian Institution in Washington, D.C., the History Museum has Lindbergh's flight jacket. The History Museum covers the time when St. Louis was the queen city of steamboating, too. Children enjoy climbing into the pilot house of the 1904 steamboat, the *Golden Eagle*.

Forest Park also has the Municipal Open-Air Theater, the nation's largest outdoor theater, which opened in 1919. Here the St. Louis Municipal Opera offers performances with visiting stars all summer long. For each performance, 1,500 of its 11,500 seats are free to the public.

The park's newest attraction is the Science Center, which is still being expanded. Its McDonnell Star Theater has a Digistar computer that makes people feel as if they are being transported through space. Hands-on exhibits in the building allow visitors to participate in activities such as making electronic music and walking through what looks like a real Missouri cave. Outside, there are more exhibits, including some almost life-size dinosaurs.

St. Louisans in the city and the county appreciate Forest Park. In the 1970s, people in both areas voted for a special tax district so that everyone could support the Science Center, the zoo, and the art museum.

Since the city of St. Louis is small,

The colorful Clydesdale horses pull a wagon at Grant's Farm.

parts of St. Louis County are just a short distance from the city boundaries. Residents of the city travel to the county to visit attractions such as Grant's Farm, the Magic House, and the National Museum of Transport.

Grant's Farm, the estate of August Busch, Jr., was named in honor of the log cabin built by President Ulysses S. Grant, another famous person who lived in St. Louis. The farm is best known as the home of the Clydesdale horses, featured on Anheuser-Busch commercials.

The Magic House specializes in hands-on exhibits for young people of all ages. Visitors can explore a maze, make their hair stand on end by holding a special ball, and feel their way through the very dark Touch Tunnel.

The National Museum of Transport has real trains and streetcars, as well as other vehicles, old and new. Here people young and old can go back in time by climbing aboard a huge old engine such as the Union Pacific's "Big Boy."

The Mississippi River is part of St. Louis County, too. At the Golden Eagle River Museum, visitors can see steamboat models and items used on real steamboats, such as the big wheel that the pilot for the *Betsy Ann* once turned and an anchor from the *River Queen*. Bee Tree Park, in which the museum is located, lies along the river and has several high lookouts that provide good river views.

In St. Louis, the river is never very far away. In the past, it played an important role in the way the city developed. Today, it contributes to St. Louis's economic and cultural life, and in the future, the river may continue to help shape this proud American city.

A girl's hair stands on end at Magic House.

Places to Visit in St. Louis

Riverfront and Nearby

Boats on levee:
  Admiral
  (314) 436-SHIP
  Entertainment center

  City of St. Louis towboat
  (314) 436-7550
  Tour, gifts, café, visitors center

  Goldenrod Showboat
  (314) 621-4040
  Theater, restaurant

  President
  Gateway Riverboat Cruises
  (314) 621-4040
  Daily cruises

  U.S.S. *Inaugural*
  300 N. Wharf Street
  (314) 421-1511
  Tour of World War II minesweeper

Busch Stadium
Between Walnut, Broadway, Spruce, and

Seventh streets
(314) 241-3900
St. Louis Cardinals, tour

Campbell House
1508 Locust Street
(314) 421-0325
Historic home, toy exhibits

Dental Health Theater
Laclede's Landing
727 N. First Street
(314) 241-7391
Giant teeth, puppets

Eugene Field House
634 S. Broadway
(314) 421-4689
Home of poet, toy exhibit

Jefferson National Expansion Memorial
11 N. Fourth Street
Between Leonor K. Sullivan Boulevard and
Memorial Drive

  Gateway Arch
  (314) 425-4465

Viewing room at top

Museum of Westward Expansion
(314) 425-4465
Exhibits, ranger programs

Old Cathedral
(314) 231-3250

Old Courthouse
(314) 425-4465
Exhibits on St. Louis history

Mercantile Money Museum
Seventh and Washington
(314) 425-8199
Exhibits on money

National Bowling Hall of Fame
111 Stadium Plaza
(314) 231-6340

St. Louis Centre
Between Washington, Locust, 6th, and 7th
streets
(314) 231-5522
Shopping, restaurants

St. Louis Sports Hall of Fame
100 Stadium Plaza
(314) 421-FAME

St. Louis Union Station
Market and 18th streets
(314) 421-6655
Shopping, hotel, restaurants

Midtown

Bob Kramer's Marionnettes
4143 Laclede Avenue
(314) 531-3313
Demonstrations, tours

Fox Theatre
527 N. Grand Boulevard
(314) 534-1678
Musical events, tours

St. Louis Symphony
Powell Hall
718 N. Grand Boulevard
(314) 534-1700
Musical events, tours

North St. Louis

Bissell Mansion Restaurant
4426 Randall Place
(314) 933-9830
Dinner mystery theater

Black Repertory Theater
240 St. Louis Avenue
(314) 231-3706

Crown Candy Kitchen
1401 St. Louis Avenue
(314) 621-9650
Ice cream, candy, food

South St. Louis

Anheuser-Busch
13th and Lynch
(314) 577-2626
Tours of brewery

Missouri Botanic Garden (Shaw's Garden)
4344 Shaw Boulevard
(314) 577-5100

Ted Drewes
6726 Chippewa; (314) 481-2652
4224 S. Grand Avenue; (314) 352-7376

Tower Grove Park
Between Grand, Arsenal, Kingshighway,
and Magnolia
(314) 771-2679

Forest Park Area

Arena
5700 Oakland
St. Louis Blues: (314) 781-5300
Hockey and other events

Jefferson Memorial Building/The History
Museum
Grand Drive
(314) 361-1424

Municipal Open-Air Theater
Theater Drive
Forest Park
(314) 361-1900
Summer musicals

St. Louis Art Museum
Fine Arts Drive
Forest Park
(314) 721-0067

St. Louis Zoo
Wells Drive
Forest Park
(314) 781-0900

Science Center
Clayton Road
Forest Park
(314) 289-4444
Planetarium, hands-on science exhibits

Steinberg Memorial Skating Rink
Jefferson Drive
Forest Park
(314) 361-5103
Roller skating in summer, ice skating in winter

St. Louis County

Dog Museum of America
Queeny Park

1721 S. Mason Road
(314) 821-DOGS
Tapes on breeds; live dogs Sunday afternoons

Golden Eagle River Museum
Bee Tree Park
(314) 846-9073

Grant's Farm
10501 Gravois Road
(314) 843-1700
Home of the Clydesdale horses

The Magic House
516 S. Kirkwood Road
Kirkwood, Missouri
(314) 822-8900
Hands-on children's science museum

McDonnell Douglas Prologue Room
McDonnell Boulevard and Airport Road
(314) 232-5421
Air and space flight exhibits

National Museum of Transport
3015 Barrett Station Road

Kirkwood, Missouri
(314) 965-7998
Old trains, buses, streetcars

Illinois

Lock No. 27 Visitors Center
West of Highway 3
Granite City, Illinois
Tows passing through lock

Additional information can be obtained from these agencies:

St. Louis Convention and Visitor's Commission
10 S. Broadway
Suite 300
St. Louis, MO 63102
(800) 325-7962 or (314) 421-1023

Jefferson National Expansion Memorial
National Park Service
11 N. Fourth Street
St. Louis, MO 63102
(314) 425-4465

St. Louis: A Historical Time Line

1764   St. Louis is founded

1804   St. Louis becomes part of United States in Louisiana Purchase (France sold the Louisiana Territory to the United States late in 1803)

1817   First steamboat visits St. Louis

1818   St. Louis University, first university west of Mississippi, is founded

1820   Missouri becomes a state

1822   St. Louis is incorporated as a city

1834   Old Cathedral is completed

1836   Lafayette Park, first public park west of Mississippi, is created

1847   Dred Scott begins his legal battle in Old Courthouse

1849   Great Fire destroys levee buildings and steamboats

1852   First railroad train travels west from St. Louis

1859   Henry Shaw founds Shaw's Garden

1874   Eads Bridge is completed across Mississippi

1876   St. Louis City and County separate; Forest Park opens

1896   Destructive tornado strikes St. Louis

1904   Louisiana Purchase Exposition

1927   Charles Lindbergh flies across the Atlantic Ocean in *Spirit of St. Louis*, paid for by St. Louis backers

1965   Gateway Arch opens to public

1985   New Union Station opens

1988   Congressman Richard Gephardt seeks Democratic nomination for president

Index